11th Street

Large-scale evacuation of cities would be needed in the event
of A-bomb or H-bomb attack....The rapid improvement of the
complete 40,000-mile interstate system, including the necessary urban connections thereto, is therefore vital as a civil-de-
fense measure.
   —*The (General Lucius D.) Clay Committee, November 1954*

11th Street

How the Interstate Highways Changed Route 66 and America's Main Street

Terry Young

Independently Published
2026

For my mother and father,
who began my life on Admiral Place
(the original Route 66!).

And for the people of Tulsa—
whose memories keep 11th Street alive.

TABLE OF CONTENTS

PREFACE

Tulsa, Route 66, and the Long Life of Public Decisions

THE WORLD OF ROUTE 66

I was born in Tulsa in 1948, when downtown still seemed permanent. On Saturdays in the early 1950s my parents took me along 11th Street—then part of U.S. Route 66—past busy storefronts with sidewalk displays, gas stations on almost every corner, and, especially, Hawks Dairy, where ice-cream cones tasted like a small celebration at the end of the afternoon. It was not only a commercial street. It was a civic place, and even a child could feel the pride that attached to it.

Along that same road stood the 11th Street drive-in theater, its tall screen rising above rows of parked cars on warm summer nights. Families came early, children in pajamas in the back seat, the smell of popcorn drifting through open windows. Travelers from farther west or east sometimes stopped there, folding an evening's entertainment into a long journey. The drive-ins were part of a roadside world of motels, diners, service stations, and neon signs—businesses that lived by the predictable flow of cars along the highway.

On 11th Street near Sheridan Road, the Will Rogers Theater—with its fifty-foot Art Deco tower—seated eight hundred moviegoers for Saturday matinees beginning in 1941. Five miles to the west, on past the smells at the Bama Pie company and the Rainbow Bread bakery, the great zigzag-Art-Deco Tulsa Public

Market, later known as the Warehouse Market, had opened in 1929 with its ornate façade and one-hundred-seventy-five-foot tower. My father, who clerked and made deliveries of freight for the Railway Express Agency could tell you the name of every building and its business from one end of 11th Street to the other. All together they marked the scale and confidence of a city that stood proudly along U.S. Route 66—the Magic City, Oklahoma's Magic Empire, America's Most Beautiful City, the Oil Capital of the World—the Tulsa of my childhood.

That world was not unique to Tulsa. Hundreds of American towns shared it. A national road passed through a local Main Street; travelers became customers; downtown banks financed new storefronts; newspapers, churches, and civic clubs grew together in a shared geography. In Tulsa the arrangement felt natural and enduring, as though the road and the town had been planned for one another.

Route 66 carried more than traffic. It was music. Nat King Cole's 1946 "Get Your Kicks on Route 66," was a huge hit and I remember my mother singing it around our home. It was Nelson Riddle's theme from "Route 66," a television series of the early 1960's. Yes, it was a TV series, too (although in four seasons, that Corvette did not make its way to Tulsa). The highway also carried names that revealed how Americans understood it. Business promoters called it "The Main Street of America," a phrase closely associated with Cyrus Avery, who saw the highway as a chain of local economies linked by travel. Writers and migrants knew it differently. In The Grapes of Wrath, John Steinbeck called it "the mother road," the path followed by Dust Bowl families seeking work and survival in California. Later, in honor of Oklahoma's favorite son, humorist Will Rogers, sections of the highway were officially named the Will Rogers Highway.

Each name described a different truth. Route 66 was a local icon, a commercial street that led to our downtown, a road of migration, and a national symbol at the same time. Understanding those meanings helps explain why its bypass by the interstate highways was felt not only as a change in traffic patterns, but as a loss in the emotional geography of American life—and why Tulsa still feels that history on 11th Street today.

THE PLANNING MOMENT

The change did not begin with neglect, nor with any sudden loss of civic confidence. It began with planning. In the years after the Second World War, American cities were urged to modernize their streets and highways to meet new expectations of mobility, safety, and national defense, not to mention jobs. Federal policy encouraged states and municipalities to think in systems rather than in individual streets, to anticipate growth, and to design roads that would carry traffic swiftly through and around cities.

In 1956, Congress passed and President Eisenhower signed legislation creating *The National System of Interstate and Defense Highways*. Cold War national defense rhetoric had helped secure support and major funding for a vast program of domestic infrastructure that created the interstate system. Tulsa responded to this national mandate as many cities did—with seriousness, ambition, and pride.

A year later, the city adopted the 1957 Tulsa Major Street and Highway Plan, a document widely praised in professional circles as among the most progressive transportation plans in the country. It laid out a network of expressways and major arterial streets intended to guide development for generations. The plan promised efficiency, safety, and the orderly expansion of a growing metropolitan region. Civic leaders embraced it as evidence that Tulsa would not fall behind the great American cities of its time.

Within that framework, alignments were drawn across maps that simplified neighborhoods into traffic corridors and land-use categories. Some of those lines later became parts of Interstate

44, redirecting through-traffic away from streets like 11th. One of I-44's offshoots, eventually known as Interstate 244, was placed across Tulsa's historic Greenwood District, an area already scarred by earlier tragedy. These decisions were not made lightly, and they were not unique to Tulsa. They reflected a planning philosophy widely accepted at mid-century, one that sought efficiency and growth, often without foreseeing the long civic shadows those lines on the map would cast.

At the time, the future still seemed orderly. Plans were adopted, praise was given, and the city believed it was preparing wisely for the decades ahead. Only later would it become clear that some of those lines would shape Tulsa's neighborhoods, finances, and thoroughfares for far longer than anyone expected.

LEARNING THE CONSEQUENCES

My understanding of these changes did not come from a single meeting or decision. It came gradually, during years in county government and later in the mayor's office, when questions of zoning, drainage, right-of-way acquisition, and property tax revenue brought the consequences of earlier planning directly into public view. Maps drawn a generation before still governed what could be built, what could not, and what might someday be taken for a road that had never yet appeared.

In 1976, as a county commissioner, I saw communities living with uncertainty created by long-planned but unfunded highway corridors. In Berryhill, west of Tulsa's corporate limits, perennial flooding from a local creek strained homes and small businesses alike. Engineers had long known that a western leg of the metropolitan highway system—first proposed in the 1957 Tulsa Major Street and Highway Plan—would channel drainage more effectively while removing a swath of housing along its path. Residents had lived with that prospect for twenty years. Yet no right-of-way had been acquired, no construction begun, and no clear timetable offered. Development halted in some places, assurances grew uncertain in others, and the absence of a decision became a decision of its own.

Nearly a decade later, in the middle of my term as mayor, a different problem arose along the projected southern leg of that same highway network. Landowners whose acreage lay in the proposed corridor pressed for zoning approval, arguing that the state had made clear the expressway would never be built. Planning officials faced a difficult choice between protecting a theoretical right-of-way and allowing immediate development. After contentious hearings, zoning was granted, subdivisions rose, and intersections became commercial centers years earlier than planners had imagined (although years late in theory). Decades afterward, when that highway corridor was revived through new financing arrangements, many of those same properties were acquired at great expense to build the road that earlier plans had anticipated.

By then I understood that the story of Tulsa's highways—and of its once-cherished place along the Mother Road—was not only about construction. It was about time, incentives, and the long reach of public decisions into the everyday geography of a city.

ON THE PURPOSE OF THIS BOOK

This book is written in the centennial year of U.S. Route 66, and Tulsa—once widely called the heart of America's Main Street—provides its central case study. The pages that follow are not a memoir, and they are not an argument against highways. They are an attempt to understand how national defense policy, local planning doctrine, and long-lived infrastructure decisions changed Route 66 and the civic world built around it.

The interstate system brought real benefits. It shortened journeys, improved safety, connected regions, and strengthened the nation's economy. Yet the same policies that encouraged speed and efficiency also redirected traffic away from streets like 11th, weakened roadside economies that depended on predictable flows of travelers, and reshaped neighborhoods in ways few planners expected. Some roads were built quickly, some slowly, some not at all, and some only after decades, when new institutions revived old plans. Each outcome left its mark on towns all along Route 66.

Tulsa's experience was not unique. From Illinois to California, communities along the highway saw similar changes—downtown stores that once depended on through-traffic declined, drive-in theaters closed, motels fell quiet, and new commercial centers arose near interchanges. What makes Tulsa distinctive is that its history contains the entire arc: the prosperity of Route 66, the ambitious planning of the 1950s, the construction of routes such as Interstate 44, the destruction and division of neighborhoods along the expressway later called Interstate 244, and the decades of uncertainty surrounding unbuilt corridors.

The purpose of this book is therefore simple: to explain how these changes happened, and what they teach us about the long life of public decisions.

—

E 11th St
S Lewis Ave

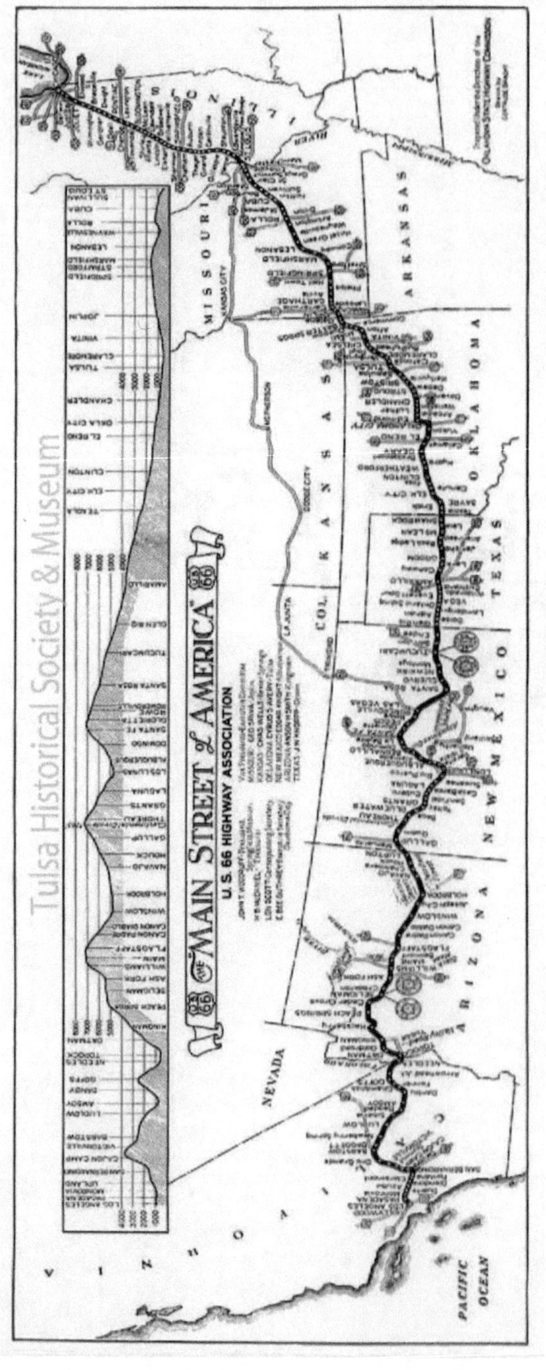

1927 Oklahoma State Highway Department Map of U.S. Route 66
(Public domain source; courtesy Tulsa Historical Society.)

CHAPTER ONE

A SATURDAY ON 11TH STREET, 1956

11th Street in Tulsa was this city's stretch of Route 66, and on Saturdays in the mid-1950s it carried the steady flow of travelers that made the road America's Main Street. Cars from Missouri and Texas mixed with Oklahoma license plates. Some drivers were passing through; others had come into town for the day. They filled parking spaces along the curb, stopped for meals, repairs, and small purchases that tied a national road to a local economy. And 11th Street led directly to Tulsa's bustling and vital downtown.

For a child, the street felt alive in ways difficult to describe later. Storefront glass reflected sunlight and traffic together. Lunch counters were crowded. And at Hawks Dairy, an ice-cream cone marked the end of the afternoon, a small ceremony repeated week after week. At night, across the intersection, the great Meadow Gold neon sign rose above 11th Street, its bright letters visible to travelers from blocks away. Erected in 1934—and today known around the world—it became one of Tulsa's enduring symbols of the roadside world.

The street was not only commercial. It was civic. People met neighbors there, greeted friends, read the headlines in newspaper racks, and spoke of school events or church meetings. Travelers who stopped for gasoline or a meal became part of the same rhythm. Route 66 brought strangers into town, but it also strengthened the sense that Tulsa belonged to a larger country moving past its doors.

Farther along the road stood a drive-in theater, one of many that served Tulsa families in the automobile age. Cars lined up at dusk, speakers hooked over open windows, children settling into the back seat while the screen brightened against the evening sky. The drive-in depended on the road as much as the diners and motels did. Its customers came from nearby neighborhoods and from travelers who found a night's entertainment along the highway. It was one more business built on the predictable flow of Route 66 traffic.

That roadside world extended beyond Tulsa to towns across the country. Motels with glowing vacancy signs, full-service gas stations with uniformed attendants, souvenir shops selling postcards and maps—all lived by the same traffic. The national road passed through local streets, and local prosperity followed it. In Tulsa the arrangement felt natural and enduring, as though the road and the city had grown together.

Yet even in 1956, lines were being drawn on planning maps that would change that world. Engineers and civic leaders were designing new expressways intended to carry traffic swiftly through and around cities. Those plans promised safety, efficiency, and preparation for national emergencies. Few people standing on 11th Street that Saturday afternoon imagined how completely those new roads would redirect the life of Route 66.

The story of 11th Street begins there—with a busy Tulsa afternoon on America's Main Street, before the highways that would pass it by had yet been built.

THE ROADSIDE ECONOMY OF ROUTE 66

Along streets like 11th in Tulsa, U.S. Highway 66 did more than carry travelers from one state to another. It sustained an entire local economy built on motion. The road's customers were not only residents. They were salesmen driving between cities, families on summer vacations, servicemen on leave, and workers moving west in search of opportunity. Each car that slowed at an intersection represented a meal purchased, a tank of gasoline filled, a room rented, or an ice-cream cone bought for a child who would remember the stop for years.

Tulsa's businesses were arranged to serve that passing trade. Service stations stood at regular intervals, some offering mechanical repair as well as fuel. Cafés advertised plate lunches and home-made pies. Motels lined the highway with rows of doors opening directly onto parking spaces. Small shops sold postcards, maps, and souvenirs bearing the number 66 in bold letters. These were modest enterprises, often family-owned, but together they formed a network that linked the national road to the local community.

Retail businesses drew neighborhood families, but it also welcomed travelers. Nearby diners and service stations benefited from the same traffic. Businesses did not compete only with one another; they depended on the same steady stream of cars. If traffic increased, all prospered. If traffic declined, all felt it.

The roadside economy required visibility and access. A traveler had to see a sign from the street, slow safely, and turn easily into a parking area. Intersections mattered. So did curb parking and storefront windows. Towns adjusted their streets to accommodate these needs, adding signals, widening lanes, and improving lighting. Municipal budgets, zoning decisions, and utility plans all assumed that the highway would continue to pass through town as it always had.

This pattern repeated across the country. In Illinois, Missouri, Texas, New Mexico, Arizona, and California, communities along Route 66 built similar businesses and expected similar results. The road was both a transportation corridor and a commercial street. Its success encouraged investment in downtown buildings, local banks, and civic institutions. Property values reflected the confidence that traffic would continue to flow past familiar storefronts year after year.

What few people recognized was how fragile that arrangement could be. The same policies that encouraged automobile travel also encouraged roads designed to avoid congestion, reduce delay, and increase speed. Limited-access highways promised safer journeys and faster commerce. When those roads were planned, they were often drawn around towns rather than through them. The decision was technical, even rational, but its consequences were profound.

On 11th Street, as on many stretches of Route 66, that realization arrived slowly. Businesses adjusted their hours, then their staff, then their expectations. Some survived by serving local customers alone. Others closed and stood vacant for years. The road still ran past their doors, but fewer cars slowed, and fewer travelers stopped. A national highway had become a local street.

The roadside economy of Route 66 was never written into law, but it shaped the daily life of towns across America. Understanding how it worked—and why it changed—is essential to understanding what happened to Route 66 itself.

THE PLANNING BEGINS

While businesses along 11th Street prospered from the steady flow of Route 66 traffic, another set of ideas was taking shape in engineering offices and planning commissions across the country. These ideas were not directed against Main Street commerce. They were aimed at problems that seemed urgent in the years after the Second World War: growing traffic, rising accident rates, and fears that the nation's roads would be unable to serve military needs in an emergency.

Automobiles were increasing faster than most cities could accommodate. Trucks carried a larger share of freight. Congestion delayed commerce and frustrated travelers. Engineers proposed new kinds of highways—roads without intersections, without curb parking, without storefront entrances—to move traffic more safely and efficiently. They promised speed and order in place of delay and confusion.

Federal policy encouraged these ideas. Cold War military planners argued that a national system of modern highways would allow rapid movement of troops and equipment across the country, as well as possible mass evacuations. Economists predicted that faster transport would reduce costs and increase growth. Civic leaders, proud of their cities and eager to keep pace with national progress, embraced the new planning philosophy. To design boldly for the future was considered responsible government.

Tulsa joined that effort with determination. In 1957 the city adopted the Tulsa Major Street and Highway Plan, a comprehensive proposal for expressways and arterial streets intended to guide development for decades. The plan was widely praised in professional circles. It promised safer travel and relief from fast-increasing congestion. It also reflected a national confidence that modern engineering could solve urban problems if cities planned ahead.

On maps prepared for the plan, lines were drawn across neighborhoods that had grown gradually over generations. Those lines were abstractions—corridors measured in feet and traffic volumes—but they overlaid real streets and homes. Some became parts of Interstates 44 and 244, which would carry through-traffic past the Route 66 corridor, although I-44 planners generously included exit ramps for 11th Street. Each alignment was justified by engineering judgment and the planning standards of the day.

At the time, few people standing on 11th Street considered what those lines might mean. The plan seemed distant, technical, and even reassuring. It suggested that Tulsa would continue to grow, that traffic would be handled safely, and that the city would keep pace with the nation's progress. Businesses along Route 66 still prospered, and the road's customers still filled parking spaces on Saturday afternoons.

Yet the new highways were designed for speed, not for storefronts. They would carry travelers past towns rather than through them. That choice, rational in engineering terms, would change the life of Route 66 in ways no planner in 1957 could fully foresee.

WHEN THE TRAFFIC MOVED

For many years after the 1957 Tulsa Major Street and Highway Plan was adopted, the life of U.S. Route 66 in Tulsa seemed unchanged. Cars still filled the curb lanes on 11th Street. Travelers still stopped for meals and gasoline. Children still counted on an ice-cream cone at Hawks Dairy after an afternoon downtown or maybe a family dinner at the Golden Drumstick. By 1960, an upstart business named Looboyles - "the store that has everything" - was *the* place to shop. The new highway plans were real alright, but they were still just lines on paper, distant from the daily rhythm of the road.

When construction began on what was originally named Skelly Drive, the change came slowly at first. Detours appeared. Earth-moving equipment stood where fields had been. New bridges rose over creeks and rail lines. Drivers curious about the new road tried it once or twice, then returned to familiar streets where they knew the cafés and service stations.

Controlled-access highways do not replace local streets overnight. They draw traffic gradually. A salesman trying to reach Oklahoma City more quickly chooses the new road. A truck driver hauling freight finds fewer stoplights along the expressway. Families heading west on vacation follow the new route marked on modern maps. Each decision seems small, but together they change the flow of cars through a city.

On 11th Street the difference appeared in small ways. Parking spaces that had once been scarce became easier to find. Restaurants shortened their hours. Motels advertised weekly rates to local workers instead of nightly rates to travelers. Service stations waited longer between customers. A drive-in theater that once filled its rows on summer weekends began to see empty spaces where cars had once stood.

None of this happened in a single season. Businesses adjusted as best they could. Some found new customers among nearby neighborhoods. Others closed quietly and were replaced by offices, warehouses, used car lots, or vacant tracts. The road still passed their doors, but fewer travelers stopped. The national highway had begun to move elsewhere.

Tulsa was not alone. All along the 2,200-miles of Route 66, towns experienced the same slow redirection of traffic. The interstate system did not abolish the old road; it made it unnecessary for long-distance travel. Where a traveler once had to pass through town, he could now pass around it. The change was efficient and often safer. It was also final.

For streets like 11th, the question was not whether the old highway would disappear—it would remain marked on maps and signs—but whether the life built around it could survive when the travelers no longer needed to use it.

WHAT REMAINED ON 11TH STREET

After traffic began to move to newer routes, 11th Street did not become silent. It became local. The same street still carried buses, delivery trucks, and the daily errands of Tulsa families. Schools, churches, and small shops continued their routines. But the stream of unfamiliar license plates grew thinner, and with it the steady flow of small purchases that had once tied a national highway to a neighborhood economy.

One of the clearest signs of the change was the roadside motel. 11th Street had once offered dozens of them, each with its own neon sign promising clean rooms and easy parking for travelers moving along U.S. Route 66. After traffic began to shift, the most familiar sight became closed motels—rows of doors locked, parking lots empty, curtains drawn in rooms that had once filled by sunset. Some owners tried to hold on by adding new promises to their signs: Cooled Air, In-Room Phones, Color TV. Each improvement reflected the standards travelers now expected on newer highways. Yet the word that grew larger and brighter on many signs was Vacancy, glowing through the evening with fewer cars turning in.

These motels had been built for movement. They depended on travelers who needed a room for a single night and a meal before continuing west or east. When the flow of long-distance traffic shifted to routes such as Interstate 44, local customers alone could not fill the rooms. Some motels became weekly rentals. Others stood empty, then deteriorated. Their neon signs went dark one by one, leaving quiet lots where headlights had once lined up at the office window.

For people who had grown up along 11th Street, the closed motels were among the most visible reminders of what had changed. They showed how closely the life of Route 66 had been tied to travelers who no longer needed to stop.

Buildings aged in place. Storefront windows that once held bright displays showed paper signs or drawn shades. Paint faded. Roofs needed repair. A property that had once been valuable because it faced a busy highway was now judged by neighborhood trade alone. Some owners kept their businesses open out of loyalty and habit. Others sold to investors who waited for better times that did not always come.

Yet memory remained strong. People who had grown up on Route 66 remembered crowded sidewalks and neon lights. They remembered the movie theater, the Saturday errands, and the taste of ice cream at the dairy. Those memories were not illusions; they were records of how the street had worked when travelers passed through town and stayed a while.

In later years, pieces of that world began to return in new forms. Preservation groups placed Route 66 markers along surviving stretches of the road. Local historians gathered photographs and advertisements. Visitors came to see what remained of America's Main Street. On 11th Street, buildings long vacant began to find new uses, new buildings were constructed, and older structures received major renovations as Tulsa's Route 66 began to reemerge.

The revival was modest, but it showed something important. Streets do not forget their history. Even after traffic has moved elsewhere, the memory of what a road once meant can guide a community toward restoration. What remained on 11th Street was not only concrete and storefronts, but a story that linked Tulsa to the larger journey of Route 66 itself.

The chapters that follow will look beyond Tulsa to other towns along the highway and then return to the planning decisions that redirected traffic away from America's Main Street. To understand what happened to Route 66, it is necessary to see both the life that once depended on it and the ideas that changed its course.

SIGNS ALONG THE ROAD

The changes on 11th Street could be read in its signs. Neon once advertised Vacancy beside bright promises of air-conditioning, telephones, or color television. Later the same signs went dark, or were painted over, or hung crooked above empty parking lots. A traveler driving slowly along the old alignment of Route 66 could see in a single mile what the redirection of traffic meant in practice.

Service stations changed their lettering as well. Hand-painted boards that had offered free maps or radiator water were replaced by smaller notices aimed at neighborhood drivers. Cafés added breakfast specials for early commuters instead of late dinners for passing families. A drive-in theater shortened its season or closed altogether. None of these decisions were dramatic; they were adjustments to fewer customers arriving from the road.

Property owners made practical choices. Some buildings were converted into offices or warehouses. Others were divided into smaller shops. A few were simply abandoned when repair costs exceeded expected income. The roadside economy had depended on visibility to travelers, and once that visibility declined, the value of those properties changed with it.

For the city, the effects appeared in quieter ways. Sales-tax receipts shifted toward new commercial centers near expressway on-off ramps. Traffic engineers redesigned signals for local patterns instead of through-traffic. Zoning boards considered different kinds of applications along 11th Street than they had a generation before. The road still mattered, but it mattered differently.

Tulsa was repeating a pattern seen in communities along the length of Route 66. In town after town, the change could be traced in motel signs, gas-station canopies, and storefront windows. The interstate system did not erase the old road; it changed the reasons people used it. Where travelers once stopped for the night, they now drove past in search of the next interchange.

Yet the memory of what those signs had meant did not disappear. People remembered where they had stayed, where they had eaten, and where their parents had taken them after an afternoon downtown. That memory would later help inspire preservation efforts and the quiet revival of parts of 11th Street. But in the years when the traffic first shifted, the dominant impression was simply of a road adjusting to a smaller role.

Understanding those signs—their promises, their changes, and their disappearance—helps explain what happened to Route 66 in Tulsa and across the country. They were small pieces of evidence in a larger story about how highways redirect not only cars, but the life built around them.

WHERE THE TRAVELERS WENT

When travelers left 11th Street, they did not disappear. They followed newer routes designed for speed and continuity, roads that became parts of Interstate 44 and other expressways linking cities across the country. The change was practical. Drivers saved time. Trucks reduced costs. Families arrived at their destinations sooner. The same journey that once required passing along 11th Street could now be made without stopping.

For the traveler, the difference was convenience. For the town left behind, it was transformation. Businesses that had depended on unfamiliar customers saw fewer strangers walk through their doors. A motel that once welcomed travelers from three states might now rent rooms to workers on weekly terms. A café that had stayed open late for passing families closed at dusk. The street still served Tulsa, but it no longer served the nation in the same way.

New commercial centers grew near where the interstate crossed major local streets. Gas stations clustered beside ramps. Chain motels and restaurants built larger buildings designed for quick access from the highway. These businesses were not the same as those along Route 66. They were arranged for drivers who intended to stop briefly and leave again, not for travelers who spent an evening in town and returned the next year.

The change was not only economic. It altered how travelers experienced the country. A journey along Route 66 had passed through towns and neighborhoods, revealing storefronts, schools, churches, and courthouses along the way. The interstates carried travelers around those places. They saw exits instead of Main Streets, signs instead of shop windows. The nation became easier to cross and harder to know.

Tulsa's experience was repeated along the length of Route 66. In Illinois, Missouri, Kansas, Texas, New Mexico, Arizona, and California, towns watched familiar traffic shift to new roads. Some communities adapted by attracting industry or tourism. Others declined. The pattern depended on local conditions, but the cause was similar: the redirection of long-distance travel.

On 11th Street, the change was gradual but unmistakable. Businesses closed or changed hands. Buildings aged. Neighborhood customers replaced travelers. The road remained, but its purpose had narrowed. What had once been a national corridor had become a local street, carrying memories of a time when the country passed by its doors.

The next chapters will look more closely at the planning ideas that led to that change—ideas rooted in safety, efficiency, and national defense—and at how cities like Tulsa adopted them with confidence. Only by understanding those plans can we understand why the life of Route 66 changed as it did.

A STREET THAT REMEMBERS

11th Street did not forget what it had been. Even after the traffic moved elsewhere, the pavement still traced the path of U.S. Route 66 through Tulsa. Old motels stood in quiet rows. Faded signs hinted at air-conditioned rooms and vacancy lights that had once burned through summer nights. Storefront windows reflected fewer cars but the same afternoon sun. The road remained, carrying the memory of a time when travelers slowed there because they had to, and because they wished to.

For people who grew up along the street, those memories were precise. They remembered Saturdays downtown, ice cream at the dairy, and a drive-in theater along the road where families gathered in parked cars to watch a film beneath the evening sky. They remembered neon signs bright against darkness and license plates from distant states. Those recollections were not sentimental inventions. They were records of how Route 66 had once worked, and how Tulsa had taken pride in its place along America's Main Street.

Years passed, and the street changed in quieter ways. Buildings were repaired or left vacant. Motels became apartments or offices. Some blocks declined and others endured. The life of the road turned inward, serving neighborhoods instead of travelers. Yet the outline of the earlier world never disappeared. Anyone driving slowly along 11th could still see the spacing of old service stations, the wide driveways of former motels, the architecture meant to catch a traveler's eye.

In recent years, unmistakable signs of renewal have appeared. Preservation groups marked the Route 66 alignment. Visitors arrived to see what remained. Old buildings found new uses. New construction drew attention as part of Tulsa's heritage saw renewal, but still a reminder of a roadside economy that had linked a national highway to a local street.

A century after Route 66 was first marked on maps, Tulsa remembers both the road and what followed it. The memory is not only nostalgic. It asks a question. How did a street that once prospered from the nation's traffic become a quieter road serving its own neighborhoods? What decisions, made with confidence and good faith, redirected the life of Route 66 and the towns along it?

To answer that question, the story must turn from neon signs and storefronts to planning tables and engineering drawings. The next chapter begins with the ideas that promised safer, faster highways for a growing nation—and that would change 11th Street more than anyone standing there in 1956 could have imagined.

—

CHAPTER TWO

In the years when Route 66 still carried travelers past Tulsa storefronts, the city was already part of a larger transportation network. Passenger trains arrived daily. Freight moved by rail and truck. Aircraft crossed the skies above town, landing at Tulsa Municipal Airport and half a dozen other airports scattered across the city. Tulsa was not a place waiting to be discovered by modern transportation. It was already shaped by it.

Passenger rail service connected Tulsa to the rest of the country in ways that had seemed permanent. Travelers boarded trains for Kansas City, St. Louis, Dallas, and points beyond. Political campaigns still relied on whistle-stop visits; in 1948, Harry S. Truman campaigned in Tulsa during his nationwide train tour, addressing crowds at Skelly Stadium while passenger rail travel still connected the city daily to the rest of the country. Freight moved overnight through the Railway Express Agency, linking Tulsa merchants to customers far beyond Oklahoma.

Tulsa was also an aviation center. During the war years and afterward, the Tulsa plant of Douglas Aircraft Company employed thousands in aircraft production and maintenance. The Spartan Aircraft Company and its School of Aeronautics trained pilots and mechanics who served in war and peace. Later, a major maintenance base operated by American Airlines at Tulsa Municipal Airport (now Tulsa International Airport) became the city's largest industrial employer. Aviation, rail, and highway together made Tulsa a transportation crossroads long before the interstate era.

Yet for most families, daily travel still took place by car along familiar streets. Route 66 carried tourists and salesmen through Tulsa's neighborhoods. Passenger trains brought visitors to Union depot. Aircraft served longer journeys for business and government. Each system had its role, and together they formed a pattern that seemed stable. Cities planned around rail stations and highway routes, confident that the balance among them would continue.

By the early 1950s, however, engineers and planners believed that balance was already out of date. Automobile traffic was increasing faster than city streets could handle. Trucks crowded two-lane highways built for lighter loads. Military planners—convinced of the Communist threat—warned that the nation's roads were inadequate for rapid movement of troops and equipment. Civic leaders across the country concluded that a new kind of highway system would be needed to meet the demands of a growing nation.

Tulsa, with its history of railroads, aviation, and Route 66 commerce, listened carefully to those arguments. The city had prospered by keeping pace with transportation change. It would soon decide to do so again.

THE NATIONAL DEFENSE HIGHWAY IDEA

By the early 1950s, the nation's transportation system appeared strained. Trucks moved a growing share of freight on roads designed for lighter traffic. Accidents rose on crowded two-lane highways. Engineers, military planners, and civic leaders began to argue that a new kind of road would be needed—one built not for intended to serve storefronts but for continuous movement across long distances.

The idea had roots in the experience of the Second World War and advanced with the advent of the Cold War. Military planners warned that the United States lacked a reliable system for rapid movement of troops, equipment, and, if necessary, masses of people. They imagined emergencies in which convoys might need to cross several states without delay. A network of limited-access highways, free of intersections and congestion, seemed a practical answer. The proposal was not aimed at towns like Tulsa, and it was not conceived as a threat to U.S. Highway 66. It was a response to fears about national defense and the demand for economic growth.

Engineers had already studied such roads. Limited-access parkways in the Northeast and Midwest had shown that traffic could move faster and more safely when cross streets were eliminated. European highways built before the war demonstrated similar principles. By mid-century, professional organizations of highway engineers promoted standards for divided lanes, controlled entrances, wide shoulders, and gentle curves designed for higher speeds. These ideas promised efficiency, safety, and predictability for long-distance travel.

Federal policy soon followed. The Federal-Aid Highway Act of 1956 authorized a national system of interstate and defense highways, funded largely through federal gasoline taxes. States would plan routes, and the federal government would provide most of the cost. The program was presented as a partnership among national, state, and local authorities—a practical effort to modernize transportation for a growing country.

Cities like Tulsa listened carefully. They had already seen the growth of railroads, aviation, and highway traffic. They knew that commerce followed transportation improvements. To civic leaders, a modern expressway system promised industrial growth, safer streets, and protection against congestion that might otherwise cripple the city's economy. The idea of bypassing crowded commercial streets was not viewed as an attack on

Main Street but as a way to separate local traffic from through-traffic for the benefit of both.

In Tulsa, planners looked at streets like 11th and saw both prosperity and danger. Route 66 carried heavy traffic past schools, churches, and storefronts. Accidents were frequent. Trucks slowed local travel. Residents complained about noise and congestion. An interstate design seemed likely to offer relief. It would carry through-traffic elsewhere while leaving neighborhood streets quieter and safer.

Few planners imagined how completely such roads would change the life of Route 66 towns. They believed travelers would still leave the highway to visit cities, dine in local restaurants, and shop downtown. They expected Main Street commerce to adapt, not disappear. The goal was modernization, not abandonment.

Yet the logic of speed carried its own consequences. A highway designed to avoid delay naturally avoided towns. Drivers who once had to pass through Tulsa could now pass around it. Each improvement in efficiency, including automobiles built to go farther on a tank of gas, made stopping less necessary. What began as—at least in part—a defense measure became an economic force, redirecting traffic patterns that had shaped towns for decades.

Tulsa's leaders embraced these ideas with confidence. They believed modern highways would secure the city's future, just as earlier generations had believed in railroads, aviation, and Route 66. Their decision reflected the spirit of progress that had guided American transportation policy for a century—and that would soon reshape 11th Street more than anyone expected.

CYRUS AVERY AND THE LOGIC OF PROGRESS

In Tulsa, no name is more closely connected with Route 66 than that of Cyrus Stevens Avery. He was a businessman, civic leader, and tireless advocate for better roads at a time when many Americans still doubted that long-distance automobile travel could be practical. Avery helped persuade state and national planners that a highway linking Chicago, St. Louis, Tulsa, Oklahoma City, and the Southwest would serve commerce and travelers alike. When Route 66 was designated in 1926, Tulsa celebrated him as its chief champion—"the Father of Route 66."

Avery's belief was simple and consistent. Good roads brought prosperity. They connected farmers to markets, merchants to customers, and towns to one another. They encouraged tourism and investment. They made travel safer. He argued for improved highways not as an end in themselves but as instruments of economic growth and civic progress. In that belief he reflected a generation that had seen railroads transform the country and expected automobiles to do the same.

Because of Avery's work, Route 66 followed a corridor that later became familiar in other forms. Roads between Tulsa and Missouri were improved repeatedly over the decades. The opening of the Turner Turnpike in 1953 and the Will Rogers Turnpike in 1957 created a modern east-west highway across much of Oklahoma along routes long associated with Route 66 travel. Those roads eventually formed major portions of Interstate 44. Avery lived to see these projects completed, and they followed the very corridor he had promoted a generation earlier.

There is no evidence that Avery regarded these improvements as a threat to his beloved old highway. He had spent his life urging better highways, wider roads, safer bridges, and more reliable routes for commerce. Route 66 itself had been an improvement over earlier roads. Turnpikes were improvements over Route 66. Interstates were improvements over turnpikes. Each stage followed the same logic of progress that Avery had embraced from the beginning.

Yet that progress carried an unintended consequence. Route 66 prospered because travelers had to pass through towns. Modern highways were designed so they would not. The qualities that made them efficient—limited access, higher speeds, fewer stops—reduced the need for travelers to enter city streets like Tulsa's 11th. Avery had helped create a national road that strengthened Main Street commerce. The next generation of highways, built in the same spirit of improvement, would redirect that commerce elsewhere.

In the eyes of planners, engineers, and civic dreamers, transportation should always become safer, more reliable, and more efficient. Avery believed that deeply because he had seen what good roads could do for farmers, merchants, and towns. His work did not end with Route 66; it helped establish a national habit of improving the ways Americans move and trade.

In that sense, Avery stands at the center of the Route 66 story—not as a figure of irony, and not as a symbol of loss, but as a reminder of a larger American faith. Each generation builds roads for its own needs, trusting that better connections will strengthen communities. Sometimes those improvements reshape the towns that welcomed them. Yet the purpose remains the same: to link people, markets, and ideas across distance.

The highways that later bypassed 11th Street were built in the same spirit that first brought Route 66 to Tulsa. Avery would have understood that impulse. He spent his life arguing that good roads were the lifeblood of a growing nation. The story of 11th Street, like the story of Route 66 itself, begins with that belief—and continues because of it.

WHY TULSA SUPPORTED THE PLAN

When Tulsa's leaders considered new highways in the 1950s, they did not believe they were abandoning Route 66. They believed they were protecting the city's future. Tulsa had grown through railroads, aviation, and motor highways. Each generation had invested in transportation improvements, confident that better connections would bring prosperity. Expanded, controlled expressways seemed the next practical step in that tradition.

Safety was the first argument. Streets like 11th carried heavy traffic past schools, churches, and storefronts. Trucks mixed with local drivers. Accidents were common. Engineers warned that two-lane and four-lane arterial roads could not safely handle the volume of traffic expected in the coming decades. Expressways promised separation of through-traffic from neighborhood traffic, fewer collisions, and more predictable travel times.

Growth was the second argument. Tulsa expected to expand. Industrial recruiters said modern highways were essential to attract factories and distribution centers. Merchants wanted better freight connections. Civic leaders feared that cities without modern expressways would lose business to those that had them. When planners presented proposals such as the 1957 Tulsa Major Street and Highway Plan, they were speaking to these concerns about economic competition as well as traffic congestion.

Planners sometimes argued that highway corridors could be coordinated with drainage and other public works, though in Tulsa the rapid pace of urban development often outstripped adequate stormwater planning, leaving neighborhoods vulnerable to flooding in ways not fully understood at the time. These difficulties were rarely intended; they reflected assumptions about growth, engineering capacity, and periodic system upgrades that proved too optimistic.

Tulsa's support for modern highways was therefore not careless. It reflected the experience of a city that had prospered by adapting to transportation change. Leaders who remembered the arrival of Route 66, passenger rail service, and aviation believed that better roads would again strengthen Tulsa's place in the region. They expected downtown commerce to remain strong while expressways carried long-distance traffic more safely around crowded streets.

Few imagined how deeply such roads would alter neighborhoods. Selected routes reshaped commercial patterns and property values across the city. These outcomes were rarely intended. They were consequences of decisions made with confidence that engineering solutions could improve urban life.

Tulsa's leaders acted as leaders in other American cities did. They relied on expert advice, federal incentives, and the belief that transportation progress would continue to bring growth. Their decision to support new highways was consistent with the same optimism that had once welcomed Route 66. It was part of a long American habit of building roads toward the future, trusting that prosperity would follow.

WHAT PLANNERS EXPECTED

When Tulsa's leaders studied proposals for new expressways, they believed the city could gain the advantages of modern highways without losing the life of Route 66. Engineers explained that limited-access roads would carry long-distance traffic more safely and efficiently while leaving neighborhood streets quieter and easier to use. Through-traffic and local traffic would be separated, each traveling where it belonged. The promise sounded reasonable and practical.

Planners expected downtown commerce to remain strong. Travelers who wished to visit Tulsa would leave the expressway at marked exits, enter the city, and return to the highway afterward. Merchants would continue to serve customers who chose to stop, and Route 66 businesses would adapt to new patterns just as they had adapted to earlier changes in automobile travel. Modern highways, it was believed, would complement Main Street rather than replace it.

They also expected that growth would follow the new roads in orderly ways. Industrial districts would locate near interchanges. Residential areas would expand where land was available. Arterial streets would connect neighborhoods to expressways without carrying the full burden of long-distance travel. The city would be easier to navigate, safer for drivers and pedestrians alike, and more attractive to investors considering where to build factories or offices. There was also an expectation that growth would proceed in an orderly way, extending only as streets, drainage, and utilities could be provided. Experience later showed how difficult it was for long-range planning to withstand the pressures for immediate development by influential landowners.

These expectations were not careless. They were based on engineering studies, traffic counts, and examples from earlier successes. Professional organizations recommended similar designs across the country. Federal incentives encouraged cities to plan boldly. Tulsa's leaders believed they were acting responsibly by preparing for a future of greater mobility and larger population.

What they did not fully foresee was how travelers would behave once new highways were built. A driver choosing the fastest route rarely leaves it without a strong reason. A truck carrying freight does not exit a limited-access road unless required. Families traveling across several states prefer efficiency over exploration. Each small decision to remain on the faster road reduces the number of travelers who enter city streets.

The result was gradual but unmistakable. Traffic that had once flowed along 11th Street moved to newer routes such as I-44 and its connecting turnpikes. Businesses that depended on passing motorists saw fewer unfamiliar customers. These changes were not part of the plan. They were consequences of the very efficiency planners had sought.

Tulsa's experience was repeated in town after town along Route 66. The expectation that travelers would leave the interstate to visit downtowns proved optimistic. Main Streets survived where local populations were large enough to sustain them, but the national stream of travelers moved elsewhere.

In the planning offices of the 1950s, few people imagined how deeply that shift would affect places like 11th Street. They believed they were improving transportation, and in many ways they were. Yet every improvement carries a direction, and the direction of the interstate highways was away from the roadside world that Route 66 had created.

WHAT THEY DID NOT FORESEE

The changes did not arrive with a single ribbon cutting. They appeared first in small ways along 11th Street with more and more empty parking spaces. New routes redirected commercial development toward new high traffic connections. This often altered property values. These outcomes were rarely intended. They were consequences of decisions made expecting engineering solutions could improve urban life.

They did not imagine how long plans would take to complete. Congressional funding delays, rising material and labor costs, and changing state highway department priorities left some routes unbuilt for decades. Land reserved for highways stood unused. Development stalled in uncertain corridors, while growth accelerated elsewhere. Communities waited for improvements that came slowly, if at all, and the geography of the city adjusted to expectations that did not always match reality.

They did not expect transportation modes would change together. Passenger rail service declined as highways expanded. Travelers who once arrived by train or Route 66 found quicker routes by car or airplane. Tulsa remained an aviation center, but the pattern of movement shifted. Each improvement in one system reshaped the others, often in ways no single plan could anticipate.

Above all, planners did not foresee that efficiency would redirect attention from streets like 11th. Route 66 would remain on maps and signs, but fewer travelers would need to stop there. The roadside economy that had grown along America's Main Street depended on necessity as much as choice. When necessity disappeared, choice alone could not sustain it.

These outcomes were not failures of intent. They were the long reach of public decisions into the daily geography of a city. Highways built for efficiency and defense achieved their purpose, but in doing so they changed the life of Route 66 towns in ways no one standing on 11th Street in 1956 could have fully imagined.

TULSA IN A NATIONAL PATTERN

What happened along 11th Street was not unique. Across the country, towns that had grown beside U.S. Route 66 and other early highways saw the same gradual redirection of traffic. Limited-access roads carried travelers past city centers rather than through them. Businesses that had depended on passing motorists adjusted, closed, or moved toward new interstate-adjacent land. The pattern appeared virtually every community along the old highway—different towns, the same quiet change.

In many places, the new highways followed corridors long established by earlier roads. Turnpikes and interstates often paralleled Route 66 because geography and commerce pointed travelers along the same general routes. In Oklahoma, roads such as the Turner Turnpike and the Will Rogers Turnpike improved east-west travel across the state before later becoming segments of Interstate 44. The new roadway did not invent a route; it accelerated it. Yet speed alone was enough to change where travelers stopped.

Cities everywhere believed they could welcome modern highways without losing their Main Streets. Many did preserve downtown commerce through strong local economies or careful planning. Others watched businesses drift toward suburban shopping centers with highway adjacency. Motels that had lined the old highway found themselves distant from travelers who no longer needed to slow for traffic lights or town limits. The roadside economy that had once seemed permanent proved dependent on patterns of travel that could change within a decade.

Tulsa's experience shared another feature with these towns: the impacts appeared unevenly. Some neighborhoods prospered near new expressways. Others declined where traffic disappeared or streets were divided. New routes redirected growth toward new suburbs. Each decision had local reasons, but together they reshaped the geography of the city.

Looking back, it is easy to see a pattern that was invisible at the time. Engineers and civic leaders across the nation were working from the same assumptions about safety, growth, and efficiency. They believed they were building a system that would serve both travelers and towns. Instead, they built a network that changed the relationship between the two.

Tulsa was neither uniquely wise nor uniquely mistaken. It acted as American cities acted, confident that better transportation would bring prosperity. In that sense, the story of 11th Street is part of a national history—a reminder that decisions made in planning rooms can alter the life of communities far beyond what anyone intended.

Long before interstates were numbered, the path across northeastern Oklahoma toward Missouri had been established by commerce, geography, and habit. Traders, railroads, and early highways all followed similar ground. When U.S. Route 66 was marked in 1926, it traced that same corridor through Tulsa and eastward toward St. Louis. The route did not appear by accident. It followed the natural lines of travel that linked cities and markets across the region.

Later roads improved that corridor rather than replacing it. The opening of the turnpikes between Oklahoma City and the Missouri state line, provided faster, safer travel along paths long familiar to motorists. The road surface changed, the speed increased, and the number of exits and entrances declined, but the direction of travel remained the same.

This continuity explains why the new highways had such power. They did not invent a new way across Oklahoma; they accelerated an old one. Travelers who once drove past motels and cafés on 11th Street now passed the same city at greater speed on roads designed to avoid delay. The choice was easy and natural. Efficiency drew traffic to the faster road, and habit soon followed.

For Tulsa, the enduring corridor was both advantage and loss. The city remained connected to the national stream of commerce, yet the businesses that had depended on Route 66 traffic saw fewer strangers at their doors. The corridor endured, but its benefits shifted in location and kind.

The same pattern appeared across the country. New highways often paralleled older ones because geography seldom changed. Rivers still needed bridges, mountains still offered only certain passes, and cities still lay where railroads and markets had placed them. What changed was speed. When travel became faster, distance shrank, and the reasons to stop along the way grew fewer.

Understanding this continuity helps explain why Route 66 declined without ever disappearing. The road remained on maps and signs. It still carried local traffic and nostalgic travelers who wished to see America's Main Street. But the national corridor it had once represented moved to roads built for a different age. Tulsa stood where it had always stood, along a path shaped by history, watching the stream of travel move a little farther from its storefronts.

The next chapter turns to how those new roads were built—the financing, engineering, and political choices that carried the interstate highway idea from drawing boards to concrete—and how their construction finally changed the life of 11th Street.

—

CHAPTER THREE

BUILDING THE INTERSTATE HIGHWAYS

By the late 1950s the idea of a national system of modern highways was no longer theoretical. Congress had authorized construction, states had begun planning routes, and engineers were
marking corridors across the country. Roads such as U.S. Highway 66 still carried heavy traffic through cities like Tulsa, but
attention had shifted to highways designed for speed, safety, and
uninterrupted travel.

Building those roads required new methods of financing
and coordination. The Federal-Aid Highway Act of 1956 created
a trust fund supported by gasoline taxes, with the federal government paying most of the construction cost. States selected
routes and supervised engineering. Cities adjusted local street
alignments to meet newly proposed major access points. It was
a partnership unlike any earlier road program, large enough to
reshape landscapes and economies across the nation.

In Oklahoma, existing turnpikes showed how modern highways could be built quickly when financing was secured. The
Turner Turnpike and the Will Rogers Turnpike demonstrated
that motorists would pay tolls for faster, uninterrupted travel
across long distances. These roads later became major portions
of Interstate 44, illustrating how older routes could evolve into
parts of the interstate system.

Construction began with surveys and land acquisition. Engineers studied soil, drainage, and traffic patterns. Rights-of-

way were purchased across farms, neighborhoods, and commercial districts. Bridges rose over creeks and rail lines. Concrete replaced gravel. Each mile required coordination among contractors, state officials, and federal inspectors. The work was technical and often impressive, a visible sign of a nation investing in its future.

In Tulsa, expressways promised relief from congestion along streets like 11th. Trucks and long-distance travelers would use faster routes around downtown, leaving major arterial streets less congested and safer for the casual traveler and locals. Civic leaders expected the new roads to bring industry and investment while preserving the life of America's Main Street through town. The logic seemed sound. Cities across the country were making similar decisions.

Yet construction itself brought change before the highways were even complete. Property values shifted along planned corridors. Businesses relocated. Neighborhoods adjusted to uncertainty about routes that might or might not be built soon. A city's geography began to change as soon as a line appeared on a planning map.

The building of the interstate highways was therefore not only an engineering project. It was a transformation of land, commerce, and expectation. Roads intended to serve a growing nation would soon alter the life of Route 66 towns in ways no blueprint could fully predict.

RIGHT-OF-WAY

Before a mile of concrete could be poured, land had to be found. Every new expressway required a continuous corridor wide enough for lanes, shoulders, drainage, and ramps. Survey crews marked property lines. Appraisers calculated values. Negotiators visited owners with maps and offers. The process was orderly on paper, but in practice it touched homes, shops, farms, and neighborhoods that had grown over decades.

Along routes that paralleled Route 66, right-of-way often crossed land already shaped by earlier roads and rail lines. Some owners sold willingly, expecting growth near the new highway. Others resisted, uncertain where they would move or how their business would survive. In cities, the process could divide streets that had once been connected and place new barriers between neighborhoods.

In Tulsa, planned corridors intersected areas of steady commercial life and established communities. Survey stakes marked paths across blocks that residents had assumed would remain unchanged. These were not abstract lines. They were yards, storefronts, churches, and schools now impersonally measured in feet and inches.

Right-of-way acquisition also carried uncertainty. Some projects moved quickly. Others were delayed by funding shortages or changes in priority. Land reserved for highways could—and did—remain undeveloped for years, waiting for construction that had not yet begun. Property owners hesitated to repair buildings or invest in improvements. Neighborhood plans paused while officials decided when or whether a road would be built.

In such conditions, development shifted toward areas with clearer prospects. Businesses relocated nearer proposed major ingress-egress points. Subdivisions grew along streets expected to connect with future expressways. The city's geography began to change before the highways themselves were complete. Decisions made in survey offices and city hall chambers altered patterns of investment across Tulsa.

These effects were seldom dramatic at first. They appeared as postponed repairs, vacant lots, or storefronts offered for sale. Yet they shaped the life of the city as surely as cured concrete.

Right-of-way was the quiet beginning of a transformation that would later be seen in traffic patterns and commercial change along streets like 11th.

For Route 66 towns across the country, the process was similar. Land was measured, purchased, and cleared for roads meant to serve national travel. When construction finally came, it followed paths prepared years earlier. The new highways did not arrive suddenly; they were preceded by decisions about land that gradually redirected the future of Main Street.

CONSTRUCTION

When right-of-way had been cleared and contracts awarded, construction began in earnest. Earthmovers cut through hills, filled low ground, and laid the broad foundations required for modern highways. Bridges rose above creeks and rail lines. Interchanges took shape where ramps curved gently to meet local streets. Roads such as Interstate 44 were designed not simply as wider highways, but as entirely new kinds of routes—roads meant to carry traffic without interruption for hundreds of miles.

The work was impressive and often admired. Photographs in local newspapers showed new bridges and wide lanes where fields or vacant land had stood. Civic leaders attended groundbreakings and ribbon cuttings. Engineers explained the advantages of divided traffic, controlled entrances, and safer curves. To many residents, the new highways represented progress in its most visible form.

Construction also brought disruption. Detours redirected traffic through neighborhoods unprepared for heavy trucks. Dust and noise lasted for months. Streets that had connected one block to another were closed or rerouted. Businesses near construction zones lost customers who found it easier to shop elsewhere. None of this was unexpected, but it reminded communities that building a highway meant more than laying concrete.

Along corridors that paralleled the old highway, construction had another effect. Drivers curious about the new road tried it before it was fully complete. Even partial segments shortened travel times. Truckers learned new routes. Families on vacation followed detour signs that led them around crowded streets. Each small shift in habit reduced the number of travelers passing along 11th Street and similar Main Streets across the country.

In Tulsa, the impact varied from block to block. Some areas welcomed easier gateways to regional travel. Others found themselves separated from familiar streets by embankments or bridges. These outcomes were rarely the intention of planners, but they were part of building roads designed for uninterrupted travel.

Construction crews measured progress in miles completed and bridges finished. Cities measured it in new traffic patterns and changing neighborhoods. When the final surface was set and the last detour sign removed, the new highways were ready to serve a growing nation. Yet their completion also marked the moment when the life of Route 66 towns began to change in ways that could no longer be reversed.

The interstate highways had been built. What followed was the quiet redirection of travelers—and with them, the commerce that had once filled streets like 11th.

OPENING THE ROAD

When the last detours were removed and the ribbon was cut, the new highways quickly filled with traffic. Drivers who had waited months to try the faster road found that trips which once required an afternoon could now be made in hours. Trucks hauling freight discovered fewer stops and more predictable schedules. Families traveling across several states learned to follow the new signs toward routes such as I-44, confident that the road ahead would be wide, smooth, and continuous.

At first, the change felt like convenience rather than trans-formation. Local drivers used the new road for errands across town. Businesses near cloverleaf and diamond access saw increased traffic. Travelers still turned toward Tulsa for meals or repairs, just as they had along Route 66. The city seemed to gain another useful road without losing the old one.

But traffic patterns shift quietly. A businessman trying to reach St. Louis before nightfall chooses the faster route. A truck driver avoids crowded streets to keep a delivery schedule. A family on vacation follows the road with fewer stops and clearer directions. Each decision seems small, yet together they reduce the number of travelers who leave the highway to enter city streets.

New centers of commerce grew where the highways met major streets. Gas stations, motels, and restaurants clustered near ramps where travelers could stop briefly without leaving their route. Shopping centers followed suburban growth encouraged by easier driving. These changes were not part of a single plan. They were the natural result of roads designed to avoid delay.

Cities like Tulsa had expected to gain modern highways and keep their Main Streets unchanged. Instead, they gained both highways and new commercial geography. The corridor endured, but its benefits shifted toward interchanges and suburbs. Streets like 11th, once part of a national journey, became primarily local roads serving their own neighborhoods.

When the interstate highways opened, they fulfilled their promise of speed and safety. They also began a quiet redirection of travel that reshaped Route 66 towns across the country. What had been America's Main Street did not disappear; it was simply no longer necessary for the nation's journey.

After the new highways opened, no announcement declared that Route 66 had entered a different era. There was no single season when 11th Street changed at once. The redirection of travel happened quietly, through choices made day after day by drivers who preferred the faster road. Each decision was reasonable. But together they reduced the stream of travelers that had once filled Tulsa's 11th Street.

The shift also altered how travelers experienced the country. Route 66 had carried motorists through towns, past storefront windows and courthouse squares. They saw schoolyards, churches, and small businesses along the way. The interstate carried them around those places. They saw exit numbers instead of street names, service plazas instead of local diners. Traversing the country was speedier, but more impersonal.

Tulsa's experience matched that of many Route 66 towns. Where travelers once had to pass through Main Street, they could now pass around it. The difference was not caused by intention but by efficiency.

Yet the old road did not vanish. 11th Street continued to serve Tulsa families. Buses ran their routes. Children walked to school. Shops opened each morning. What changed was the road's place in the national journey. It had been part of a coast-to-coast highway. It became a city street that remembered when the country had passed its doors.

The quiet redirection of travel was the true turning point. Highways built for speed did exactly what they were meant to do. In doing so, they changed the life of Route 66 towns in ways no ribbon cutting had announced, but that every part of Main Street eventually felt.

When long-distance traffic moved elsewhere, streets like 11th did not disappear. They settled into a quieter role. The signs still marked the path of Route 66 through Tulsa, and neighborhood life continued along its sidewalks. Children walked to school. Churches filled on Sundays. Small shops opened their doors each morning. First run movies still played at the Will Rogers Theater. The road remained part of the city even as it ceased to be part of the nation's journey.

The federal designation of U.S. Highway 66 was terminated on June 27, 1985. Ironically, I was mayor of Tulsa on that date and I can say that, sadly, it came and went essentially unnoticed.

What remained was a roadside world built for another pattern of travel. Motels stood in rows along the highway, their doors facing parking spaces once filled each evening. Some became weekly rentals. Many were abandoned, their neon signs dark, their paint fading in the sun.

Buildings along 11th Street aged with the traffic that passed them. Storefront windows showed different goods. Parking lots were easier to enter. The sense of a national road was replaced by the pace of a city street. Yet the memory of what the road had been lingered in the spacing of driveways, the wide setbacks of old motels, and the architecture designed to catch a traveler's eye.

In time, pieces of that earlier world began to attract attention again. Preservation groups marked surviving stretches of Route 66. Visitors came to see what remained of America's Main Street. Old buildings found new uses, albeit after half a century, but still a reminder of how closely the road had been tied to everyday life in the city.

Tulsa's experience was shared by towns across the country. Some found new prosperity at major interstate junctions. Others struggled with empty storefronts and declining property values.

Everywhere, the same question appeared: what becomes of a Main Street when travelers no longer need to pass through it?

The answer was not simple. What remained on 11th Street was both loss and continuity. The road no longer carried the nation's traffic, but it still carried the memory of a time when it had. That memory would later inspire preservation and revival, but in the years when the highways first opened, it was simply a quiet reminder of how the geography of a city can change while its streets remain in place.

THE LONG VIEW

The building of modern highways did not end the story of Route 66. It began a longer chapter in which cities and towns learned to live with the systems they had built. Streets that once carried national traffic became local arteries. Commercial districts shifted toward interchange-driven development tracts. Neighborhoods adjusted to new patterns of movement. These changes unfolded slowly, often over decades, as communities discovered the lasting reach of decisions made in planning rooms years earlier.

In Tulsa, the results were uneven. Some areas prospered near routes that later formed parts of Interstate 44. Other neighborhoods faced quieter streets and declining property values where travelers no longer stopped. Each outcome had its own local history, yet together they revealed how infrastructure shapes a city's geography for generations.

Over time, communities reconsidered what had been gained and what had been lost. Looking back across decades, the pattern becomes clearer. Transportation systems rarely stand still. Cow paths and wagon trails gave way to railroads, railroads to highways, highways to interstates. Each step promises efficiency and growth. Each step leaves marks on the places it passes. The story of Route 66 is not only about one road; it is about how a nation chooses to move and how those choices shape the towns along the way.

The chapters that follow will turn from construction to experience—how Tulsa lived with its new highways, how plans were delayed or revised, how neighborhoods adapted, and how the city learned lessons from changes that took years to understand. Only by seeing those long effects can we understand what happened to 11th Street and to Route 66 across America.

LOOKING BACK FROM 11TH STREET

From the vantage point of 11th Street, the history of Route 66 can be read not only in old photographs but in the spacing of buildings and the memories of those who grew up along its sidewalks. The road that once carried travelers from Chicago toward the Pacific still runs through Tulsa, yet its role has changed. Where license plates from distant states once lined the curb, neighborhood traffic now sets the rhythm of the day.

The change did not come because Tulsa lost its place on the map. The city remained connected to the national corridor through Interstate 44. Freight still moved. Travelers still passed nearby. What changed was where they stopped. Modern highways allowed them to continue on without delay.

Yet something important endured. The buildings that lined 11th Street remained as markers of an earlier roadside economy. Old motels, service stations, and storefronts spoke quietly of the years when Route 66 was America's Main Street. Their survival was not planned. It was the result of time passing more slowly than change.

In recent years, Tulsa has begun to look again at that inheritance. Preservation efforts, new businesses, and renewed interest in Route 66's centennial have brought attention back to 11th Street. Visitors come to see what remains, and residents rediscover places that had long seemed ordinary. The revival is careful and incomplete, but it shows that history can return to streets that remember it.

Looking back from 11th Street also brings a larger understanding. The highways that redirected traffic were built for reasons that seemed urgent and sensible at the time. They improved safety, shortened travel, and strengthened commerce. They also changed the life of towns along the old road in ways no one fully intended. That is the nature of public decisions made for a growing nation.

The story now turns to how Tulsa lived with those changes—how plans were delayed, how neighborhoods adjusted, and how the city learned lessons from decades of experience. Only by following that longer history can we understand not only how Route 66 declined, but how communities began, slowly, to rediscover its value.

—

CHAPTER FOUR

LIVING WITH THE PLAN

When the new highways were opened and traffic patterns settled, Tulsa did not simply move on. The city began living with a transportation system that had been planned years earlier. Lines drawn on maps in the 1950s continued to shape land use, investment, and neighborhood expectations long afterward. Streets like 11th adjusted quietly to their new place in the city.

Some projects advanced quickly. Others did not. Funding shortages, changing priorities, and rising construction costs slowed parts of the 1957 Tulsa Major Street and Highway Plan. Corridors reserved for future highways remained undeveloped for decade after decade. Property owners hesitated to improve buildings that might later be removed. Businesses postponed expansion while waiting for decisions that seemed always to be coming soon.

The uncertainty affected whole communities. In areas west of Tulsa, residents waited sixty years for improvements that had been promised in earlier plans. Development paused while agencies debated schedules and funding. Streets were built to meet highways that had not yet appeared. The geography of the city adjusted to expectations that were never quite fulfilled.

Elsewhere, growth moved ahead without waiting. Subdivisions spread into open land beyond earlier city limits. Commercial centers appeared near roads expected to carry future traffic.

When plans changed or projects were delayed, those patterns became permanent. The city expanded in ways no single plan had intended.

Through all of this, the memory of Route 66 remained. Businesses along 11th Street continued to serve local customers. Old motels and service stations found new uses. Others waited quietly for attention that might not come for years. The road still ran through Tulsa, even as its role in the national journey had faded.

Living with the plan meant learning how long public decisions endure. A highway proposed in one decade might not be built until another. A neighborhood divided by construction might remain changed for generations. A street that once prospered from national traffic might find new life—only slowly. These were lessons Tulsa shared with towns across America as they adjusted to highways that had been designed with confidence but built over time.

The story of 11th Street did not end when traffic moved to faster roads. It entered a new phase, shaped by delays, revisions, and the everyday choices of a growing city.

WHEN PLANS FELL BEHIND

By the mid-1970s it had long become clear that parts of Tulsa's highway system were far behind the expectations of the 1957 Tulsa Major Street and Highway Plan. Projects that planners had assumed would be complete within a decade remained unfinished after twenty years. Funding had not flowed as anticipated. Construction costs rose faster than budgets. Corridors reserved for future roads stood undeveloped, while traffic increased on streets never meant to carry it.

These delays were not unique to Tulsa. Across the country, cities discovered that building modern highways required more time and money than early estimates suggested. Inflation, environmental reviews, and changing priorities slowed projects once thought inevitable. Yet in Tulsa the effects were especially visible because the city had planned aggressively for growth and had reserved land in expectation of rapid construction

The effects of delay were experienced in the community of Berryhill, just outside the western Tulsa city limits, for example, where a small, but notorious creek overflowed perennially, often several times a year, into area homes. Residents had long been told that a planned western leg of the metropolitan highway system would improve drainage and reduce flooding. The route had been approved, mapped, and discussed for years, yet even right-of-way acquisition had not begun. Property owners waited while development stalled and uncertainty grew.

The problem was not a lack of planning but a failure of execution. Funding did not arrive when expected, priorities shifted, and agencies hesitated to commit resources to a project some suggested was a pipe dream. As costs rose, construction seemed less likely, and the community endured both flooding and the economic burden of land held in reserve for a highway that did not come.

Decades later, in 2024, that western corridor was finally completed as a toll road by the Oklahoma Turnpike Authority, long after the original plan had promised relief. By then the geography of Berryhill had already been shaped by years of delay. The episode showed how infrastructure plans, even when well intentioned, can affect communities not only when they are built, but when they are postponed.

Elsewhere in the city, growth pressed ahead without waiting. Subdivisions appeared near roads expected to connect with future expressways. Commercial centers opened at intersections that planners had once intended for quieter use. When projects were delayed, these patterns became permanent. Streets designed for through-traffic became local commercial strips.

Neighborhoods adjusted to decisions made by necessity rather than design.

Along 11th Street, the contrast was plain. Traffic that once filled the road had shifted to newer routes. Elsewhere, planned improvements meant to connect neighborhoods and relieve congestion remained incomplete. The city lived with both change and delay, adapting as best it could to a transportation system that had not arrived on schedule.

These years taught a difficult lesson. A plan drawn in confidence does not guarantee construction in time. Cities must live with uncertainty, balancing growth against expectations that may take decades to fulfill. Tulsa learned that lesson slowly, as neighborhoods waited for roads that came late—or, as the result of litigation, not at all—and streets like 11th adjusted to a future that arrived unevenly.

The unfinished parts of the plan would shape Tulsa's geography as surely as the highways that were built, reminding the city that infrastructure decisions can echo across generations long after the first line is drawn on a map.

WHEN PLANS COLLIDED WITH GROWTH

As some highway projects lagged behind schedule, Tulsa continued to grow. Subdivisions expanded into open land south and east of the city. Commercial strips appeared where traffic was expected. Schools, churches, and shopping centers were built to serve neighborhoods that had once been farmland. Much of this development followed streets intended to connect eventually with routes proposed in the 1957 Tulsa Major Street and Highway Plan. Yet uncertainty about those projects created conflict. Landowners sought permission to build in corridors long reserved for future highways. Local planners warned that such development would make future construction more expensive or impossible, while state officials were actually saying that the projects would not be built soon, or at all. City officials faced pressure from both sides—residents who wanted roads completed and owners who wanted to use their land.

In south Tulsa during the mid-1980s, large tracts of undeveloped land lay in the path of a planned southern expressway shown in the 1957 Tulsa Major Street and Highway Plan. Because state transportation officials indicated the road would not be built in the foreseeable future, landowners pressed for residential and commercial zoning in the proposed right-of-way. After contentious hearings, zoning was approved and subdivisions spread across land long reserved for the highway. The decision seemed reasonable at the time: housing was needed, the expressway appeared uncertain, and the city was growing rapidly.

Years later, when transportation priorities changed, the same corridor—like a phoenix—arose from the ashes. Property that had once been vacant had to be purchased at far greater expense. Homes were removed, businesses relocated, and portions of the route were eventually constructed as toll facilities through the Oklahoma Turnpike Authority. What might have been straightforward a generation earlier became costly and difficult, showing how uncertainty can magnify the long-term consequences of infrastructure planning.

This pattern appeared in many cities, not only Tulsa. Growth rarely pauses for long-term plans, and plans rarely anticipate every change in economy or population. Where development outpaced planning, the cost of building highways increased. Where planning outpaced development, land stood unused and neighborhoods waited.

The collision between plans and growth taught another lesson: transportation systems are built over decades, but cities change every year. Balancing those two rhythms proved harder than planners in 1957 could have imagined.

Highways are drawn as lines on maps, but when they are built they become edges in the life of a city. In Tulsa, some of the most lasting effects of the new expressways appeared not in traffic counts but in neighborhoods divided by embankments, bridges, and cul-de-sacs. Walking routes changed. Familiar paths became longer or disappeared altogether. Streets that had once connected blocks were cut short.

Among the buildings taken for the Crosstown Expressway, later I-244, was an apartment house on Admiral Place where my parents had lived when I was born and which my grandfather managed. My parents had moved by 1951, but my grandparents remained there until they had to relocate when the structure was condemned for demolition as part of the highway corridor. Their experience was not unusual; similar removals occurred across Tulsa and in cities throughout the country. Highway construction alters land use, but it also changes the geography of families.

As earlier discussed, Interstate 244 also further divided Tulsa's historic Greenwood District, a community already marked by earlier catastrophic losses. Blocks that had been rebuilt to form a single neighborhood were again separated, this time by concrete and steel. Residents adjusted as best they could, but connections that had taken years to restore were altered in essentially a single construction season. Only after the centennial observance of the Tulsa Race Massacre in 2021 did serious discussions of remediation begin, and their results remain quite uncertain.

These outcomes were not unique to Tulsa; cities across the country experienced similar divisions when new highways were routed through established neighborhoods.

Planners in the 1950s believed expressways could relieve congestion and encourage growth without lasting harm to community life. In many cases they underestimated how strongly streets and neighborhoods were linked. A bridge might replace a crossing, but it could not replace the habit of walking to a nearby store or visiting a neighbor across the street. When a familiar route was removed, the loss was measured not only in distance but in daily experience.

Some neighborhoods were clear beneficiaries, however. Businesses flourished and property values rose along certain corridors. Yet other areas found themselves quieter and less connected. Shops closed when traffic disappeared. Schools drew students from smaller areas. The pattern of daily life shifted in ways that were rarely part of any original plan.

Along 11th Street, the change was different but related. The road was not divided by an expressway, yet it lost the stream of travelers that had once tied it to the rest of the country. Its businesses served local customers instead of visitors from distant states. The effect was quieter than a bulldozer, but it was no less lasting.

These dividing lines, visible and invisible, became part of Tulsa's geography. They reminded the city that transportation decisions shape more than traffic flow. They shape how neighbors meet, how businesses survive, and how communities remember their past.

WHAT THE CITY LEARNED

Over time Tulsa began to understand that transportation plans, once adopted, shape a city for generations. Highways that seemed distant when drawn on maps determined where neighborhoods grew, where businesses invested, and how streets were used long after their designers had left public office. Streets like

11th showed how quickly a national road could be viewed as a strictly local one, and how slowly a city adjusts to that change.

The first lesson was that infrastructure decisions last longer than the expectations behind them. Plans assumed that projects would be completed within a decade, yet some routes took thirty, forty, even sixty years to finish. Land reserved for highways stood idle. Development shifted around corridors that remained uncertain. When construction finally came, it often arrived in a city different from the one planners had imagined.

A second lesson was that transportation systems affect one another. Passenger rail service declined as highways expanded. Aviation continued to grow at facilities such as Tulsa International Airport as the smaller airports disappeared, changing patterns of long-distance travel. Freight moved increasingly by truck along routes later designated as an interstate highway. Each improvement in one system altered the balance among the others, often in ways no single plan could predict.

A third lesson concerned neighborhoods. Roads intended to relieve congestion sometimes divided communities or redirected commerce toward new centers. These outcomes were rarely intended, but they showed how infrastructure decisions reach beyond traffic counts into the daily life of a city.

Yet Tulsa also learned that cities can adjust. Over the years, planning methods improved, public hearings expanded, and agencies coordinated their work more carefully. Tulsa adopted stronger approaches to land use and infrastructure management, including nationally recognized stormwater management planning that reflected lessons learned from earlier decades of rapid growth and disaster recovery. These efforts did not erase past decisions, but they showed that a city can respond thoughtfully to experience.

Along 11th Street, renewal came slowly. Some buildings were restored. Preservation groups marked the Route 66 alignment. Visitors arrived to see what remained of America's Main

Street. The revival was modest at first, but in the last decade has blossomed into a full-scale revival. This effort reflects a slow-to-mature understanding of how the city's past could shape its future.

The lessons Tulsa learned were not unique. Towns across the country discovered that highways built for speed could change Main Street, that plans could take decades to complete, and that communities must live with the results of decisions made in another time. In that sense, the story of 11th Street is part of a national history—a reminder that public works are never only about engineering. They are about the lives that unfold along the roads they build.

WHAT ENDURED ON 11TH STREET

Through all the years of planning, delay, construction, and adjustment, 11th Street remained. The pavement that once carried coast-to-coast travelers still marked the path of U.S. Route 66 through Tulsa. Buses ran their routes. Children walked to school. Churches opened their doors on Sundays. The street continued to serve the daily life of the city even as its place in the national journey had faded.

What endured most clearly were the buildings shaped by another era of travel. Old motels lined the road with parking spaces facing their doors. Service stations stood at familiar intervals. Storefronts were set back from the curb to catch the eye of passing motorists. Some of these places found new uses. Others stood vacant for years while Tulsa grew around them.

The structure that once housed Hawks Dairy remained one of those reminders. For decades it has stood as a memory of Saturday afternoons and ice-cream cones, part of a roadside economy that had depended on travelers moving through town. Nearby, former motels showed signs advertising cooled air or color television long after the travelers they hoped to attract had found quicker routes along roads such as Interstate 44. Their faded paint and darkened neon spoke quietly of a different time.

Yet endurance was not only physical. Memory endured as well. Families who had grown up along 11th Street remembered crowded sidewalks and license plates from distant states. They remembered drive-in theaters, Saturday errands downtown, and the pride of living in a city that stood along America's Main Street. Those recollections were records of how Route 66 had once worked and how Tulsa had taken its place within a national road.

What endured on 11th Street was not only brick and mortar. It was the understanding that transportation decisions shape communities long after construction crews leave. A road that once carried the nation can become a local street, yet still hold the memory of what it meant to be America's Main Street.

Tulsa learned that lesson slowly. Plans drawn in confidence reshaped neighborhoods, redirected commerce, and altered the expectations of a growing city. Some changes brought growth; others brought loss. All of them showed that highways are never only engineering projects. They are decisions about how a city will live.

The story of 11th Street does not end with the completion of the highways. It continues in the choices Tulsa makes today about preservation, development, and memory. That continuing story—how a road once at the center of a national journey lives in a new century—is the subject of the next chapter.

—

CHAPTER FIVE

11 BY 66

11th Street did not disappear when traffic moved to faster roads. It waited—quietly, locally, patiently—until the country remembered why Route 66 mattered.

For many years after the interstates opened, 11th Street served the ordinary work of a city. Buses ran their routes. Children walked to school. Churches opened their doors on Sundays. Neighborhood shops kept familiar hours. The old roadway that had once carried coast-to-coast travelers still marked the path of U.S. Route 66 through Tulsa, even when few travelers noticed.

The street did not lose its memory. Successive generations remembered. Those memories were not nostalgia alone. They were records of how Route 66 had once tied Tulsa to a national journey.

For a long time, that memory was quiet. Buildings changed hands. Businesses opened and closed. Blocks adjusted to neighborhood needs. The road became local because that was what the city required.

Yet the street endured in ways that were easy to overlook. Construction and infrastructure still reflected an era of motor travel. Setbacks of old motels showed how rooms had once opened toward headlights arriving from distant states. Corner buildings still turned toward passing traffic. Architecture meant to catch the traveler's eye remained long after the traveler had chosen another road.

Tulsa did not set out to preserve Route 66. It simply continued to live with the street it had.

Across the country, people began to look again at Route 66—not as a transportation system, but as a story. Historians traced its alignment through old maps. Tulsa's best-selling author Michael Wallis penned what is considered the definitive chronicle, *Route 66: The Mother Road* (1990). Photographers documented roadside architecture. Preservation groups placed markers along surviving stretches of Main Street. Travelers began to seek the old road deliberately. Tulsa discovered that it had kept more of that history than many cities. The long straight reach of 11th Street still showed the pattern of a roadside economy. The building that had housed Hawks Dairy stayed in place and old storefronts remained along the corridor, waiting quietly for attention to return. Even the decommissioned 11th Street bridge across the Arkansas River became a museum-like attraction.

As the old route approached its ninetieth year—after decades of boarded windows and abandoned buildings—the heart of America's Main Street began to stir again.

A Tulsa institution founded in 1908 – Ike's Chili – moved to 11th Street in 2014 and continues its more than century-old tradition.

In 2017, the Buck Atom Space Cowboy statue rose beside a restored 1950s filling station on 11th Street, followed in 2024 by Space Cowgirl Stella Atom. Other roadside figures and murals soon appeared, reminders that Route 66 had once celebrated motion with bright signs and bold symbols.

The Scrivner-Stevens Grocery building, built in 1939, was restored by the Lobeck Taylor Family Foundation and reopened in 2018 as Mother Road Market, Oklahoma's first nonprofit food hall, bringing new life to a landmark that had served Tulsa shoppers for many generations.

And the fully restored Meadow Gold sign—long a symbol of Tulsa's Route 66 heritage—was placed at Cyrus Avery Centennial Plaza, where its neon lights shine proudly each night.

Many Tulsans now bring their grandchildren to 11th Street to show them where Saturday afternoons once ended with an ice-cream cone and a neon sign glowing against the sky.

That is the meaning of "11 by 66:"

A Tulsa street shaped by a national road.

A national road remembered through a Tulsa street.

The journey of Route 66 through Tulsa did not end when traffic moved to faster highways. It entered another century, waiting for a time when Americans would again look for the places where their country once met itself along the road.

—

About the Author

Terry Young was born and raised in Tulsa and has spent a lifetime watching the city change—first from the sidewalks of downtown in the 1950s, later from public office, and always as a student of its history. He served as a Tulsa County Commissioner from 1976 to 1984, as Mayor of Tulsa from 1984 to 1986, and later as Managing Director of the Oklahoma Turnpike Authority, where questions about roads, growth, and public decisions became part of daily work.

Young is the author of *More Perfect, Domestic Tranquility*, and *The Error of Good Feelings,* historical studies exploring how different choices might have shaped American constitutional life. With *11th Street — How the Interstate Highways Changed Route 66 and America's Main Street*, he turns to the road he knew as a boy—the diners, neon signs, drive-ins, and license plates from distant states—to examine how interstate highways reshaped Route 66 and America's Main Street, and how Tulsa still lives with those decisions.

He continues to write and research local and national history from Tulsa, where the stories of 11th Street remain close to home.